Let's Rock!

Written by Jeanne Willis
Illustrated by Andy Rowland

Jas and Will went
to a rock gig.

Let’s be in a band!

I can rock!

I can drum!

Can I be in the band? Pick me!

“Jack has a sax!
Jack can be in the band.”

Let's rock!

Pluck! Biff!

Stop the din!

It's a rock band, Mum!

Mum grins.
"Can I be in it?"

No! Mums can not be in bands!

Mum has a van.

The band can go to gigs in the van.

Mum rocks!